Smash

summer 2001

International MUSIC Publications

© International Music Publications Limited
Griffin House 161 Hammersmith Road London W6 8BS England

Published 2001

Editorial & Production: Anna Joyce
Cover Design: Space DPS Limited

Back Here

words and music by

Christian Burns, Mark Barry, Stephen McNally and Phil Thornalley

highest chart position **5**
release date **Monday 12th February 2001**
did you know **This song stayed in the US Top 20 for over three months and received a Radio Music Award nomination for the most requested track on American radio**

1. Ba - by, set me free from this mi - se - ry; I can't take it no more.—
2. So I told you lies, ev - en made you cry; ba - by, I was so wrong.

Since you ran a - way, no - thing's been the same; don't—
Girl, I pro - mise you, now my love is true; this—

know what I'm liv - ing for.—
is where my heart be - longs.—

Here I am— so a - lone,

Chase The Sun

highest chart position **5**

release date **Monday 29th January 2001**

did you know **This dance collective is comprised of two writer/producer duos from Italy - Souled Out (who produced the 1997 Karen Ramirez hit 'Looking For Love') and Kama Sutra**

words and music by

Alessandro Neri, Marco Baroni, Domenico Canu, Sergio Della Monica and Simon Duffy

I'm fly-ing a-way,— run-ning like the— wind— as I chase the— sun!—

Up spin-ning a - round,— cir - cles in my— mind,— sail-ing ov - er - ground.

A na num na_____ yee___ yee hee._____

I'm fly-ing a-way,___ run-ning like the___ wind___ as I chase the___ sun!___

Chemistry

words and music by
Dan Wilson

highest chart position **35**
release date **Monday 19th February 2001**
did you know **The band began life as Trip Shakespeare, comprising Dan and John
with two other members (including Dan's brother Matt)
which then morphed into a band called Pleasure and eventually became
Semisonic after another band called Pleasure threatened legal action over the name**

1. I re-mem-ber when I found out a-bout che-mi-stry; it was a long,— long
2. Some time la-ter I met a young gra-du-ate when I had no-bo-dy to

way from here. I was old— e-nough to want it, but young-er than I want-ed to be;
call my own. I told her I was look-ing for some-bo-dy to ap-pre-ci-ate, and I

Verse 3:
So when I find myself alone and unworthy
I think about all the things I've learned
From the fine, fine women with nothing but good intentions
And a bad tendency to get burned.

Oh, oh, all about chemistry etc.

Always Come Back To Your Love

highest chart position **3**
release date **Monday 19th February 2001**
did you know **Samantha attended The Billy Barry Stage School at the same time as Brian from Westlife**

words and music by

Hallgeir Rustan, Tor Erik Hermansen and Mikkel Eriksen

Don't Tell Me

words and music by

Mirwais Ahmadzaï, Madonna Ciccone and Joe Henry

highest chart position 4
release date **Monday 27th November 2000**
did you know **This single has sold more than half a million copies in the USA, an achievement which puts her in joint second place, level with The Beatles, for having the most gold-status singles in chart history (this is her 24th). Elvis is still miles ahead with 51 gold singles**

1. Don't tell me to stop.____
2. *See additional lyrics*

Tell the rain not to drop,____   tell the wind not to blow_

Verse 2:
Tell me love isn't true,
It's just something that we do.
Tell me everything I'm not,
But please don't tell me to stop.
Tell the leaves not to turn
But don't ever tell me I'll learn.
Take the black off a crow,
But don't tell me I have to go.

I Can't Deny It

words and music by
Rick Nowels and Gregg Alexander

highest chart position **26**
release date **Monday 12th March 2001**
did you know Like Luciano Pavarotti, Julio Iglesias and various other musical luminaries, Rod originally began a career in football as an apprentice professional (at Brentford FC) before setting his sights on becoming a renowned singer in the early 60s

1. How can I tell you how much I love you never put no one above you.
2. How high a number, how much I dig ya oh babe there ain't no figure.

Dance With Me

words and music by
Richard Adler and Jerry Ross

highest chart position **10**
release date **Monday 12th February 2001**
did you know **Debelah can speak (and sing!) in six languages other than English: Latin, French, Portuguese, Italian, German and Hindi**

Oh come and dance with me my

ba - by. Let's dance 'til we go cra - zy. The night is young and

so are we. Let's make love____ and dance the night a - way. What I real - ly

Falling

highest chart position 11
release date **Monday 15th January 2001**
did you know **This single was only 47 single sales away from entering the UK Top 10 in its week of release**

words and music by

Lucas Secon, Keith Cox, Gary Lloyd and Chardel Rhoden

He Don't Love You

words and music by
Steve Mac and Wayne Hector

highest chart position **18**
release date **Monday 26th February 2001**
did you know Whilst band-members Andrew and Michael have collaborated with
ex-Take That frontman Gary Barlow on other material, this single
was written and produced by Steve Mac, the man behind Westlife hits
'Swear It Again', 'Flying Without Wings' and 'What Makes A Man'

If you were my girl,___ I'd give you it all.___ Why can't you

see that___ he's fak - ing?___

Make your mind up___ what you wan-na do; He don't love you, no.___

D.%. al Fine

He Loves You Not

highest chart position 17
release date Monday 5th March 2001
did you know This all female quartet was put together by US rap/hip-hop mogul
Puff Daddy (soon to change his name to 'P.Diddy'!!)
and the song was penned by the team behind
Christina Aguilera's smash hit debut single 'Genie In A Bottle'

words and music by
Pamela Sheyne, David Frank and Steve Kipner

Give it all girl, give it all you got. If you take a chance on se-cond hand shot.

Say what you want girl, do what you do. He's nev-er gon-na gon-na make it with you.

Jaded

words and music by

Steven Tyler and Marti Frederiksen

highest chart position **13**
release date **Monday 5th March 2001**
did you know **The rock legends were inducted into the Rock & Roll Hall of Fame in March 2001 after an amazing 31 years in the business**

I'm Like A Bird

highest chart position 5
release date Monday 26th February 2001

did you know This 20 year old Canadian has an eclectic heritage:
her parents are from Portugal, she can play the guitar, ukulele
and trombone and can sing in English, Portugese and Hindi

words and music by
Nelly Furtado

Repeat to fade

If That Were Me

words and music by

Melanie Chisholm and Rick Nowels

highest chart position **18**

release date **Monday 27th November 2000**

did you know **Being a Liverpudlian, Melanie is an avid supporter of Liverpool FC and it is alleged that she buys only RED toothbrushes to show her allegiance to the club**

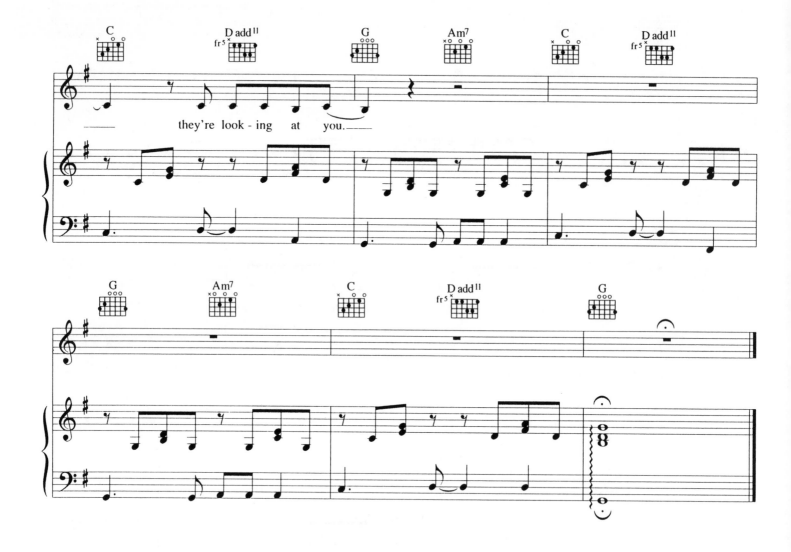

they're look-ing at you.

Verse 2:
A spare bit of change is all that I give
How is that gonna help when you've got nowhere to live?
Some turn away so they don't see
I bet you'd look if that were me.

How did you fall?
Did you fall at all?
Is it lonely where you are, sleeping in between parked cars?
When it thunders where do you hide from the storm?

Verse 3:
Could you ever forgive my self-pity?
When you've got nothing and you're living on the streets of the city
I couldn't live without my phone
But you don't even have a home.

How did we fall?
Can we get up at all?
Are we happy where we are on our lonely little star?
When it's cold is it your hope that keeps you warm?

I Need You

words and music by
Ty Lacy and Dennis Matkosky

highest chart position 13
release date **Monday 19th March 2001**
did you know LeAnn can boast two Grammys, three Academy of
Country Music Awards, a CMA 'Horizon Award',
four Billboard Music Awards and a prestigious BBC
'Rising Star' award to her name – all by the tender age of 18!

I don't need a lot___ of things, I can get by with no - thing.
You're the hope that moves___ me to___ cour - age a - gain, oh yeah.

Never Had A Dream Come True

highest chart position **1**
release date **Monday 27th November 2000**
did you know **This single, released in aid of the BBC's Children In Need appeal, shot to number 1 after first week sales of 144,000 units, which was 20,000 more than their previous single 'Natural' had sold in total up to then!!!**

words and music by
Cathy Dennis and Simon Ellis

Inner Smile

words and music by
**John McElhone, Sharleen Spiteri,
Rick Nowels and Gregg Alexander**

highest chart position **6**
release date **Monday 8th January 2001**
did you know **The band were inspired by the 1984 Wim Wenders film
'Paris, Texas' and the accompanying soundtrack
(composed and performed by slide-guitar specialist
Ry Cooder) when deciding on their name**

Moderately

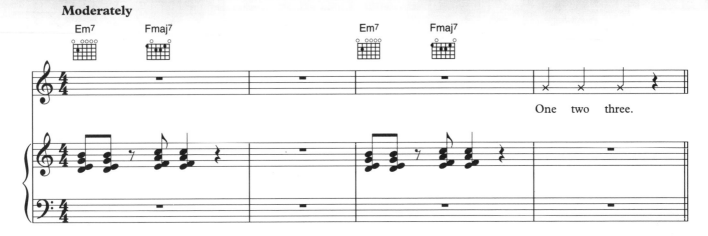

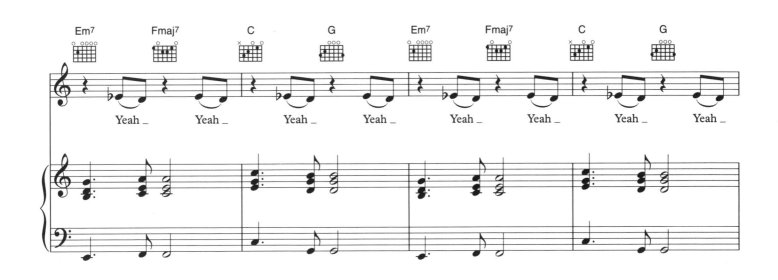

some -thing like lov -ing, and took me in too soon, you took my feel -ings from no -thing, came_
wish -es as much as your kis - ses make me blue. You've found my riv - er now will you es -

_back at__noon. Just may -be I'm rea -dy to show my -self to you.__ So if I lose_ my pa-
cape a -way_ too? But may -be I'm rea -dy I'm fall -ing in -to you.__

tience you must try_____ to un -der - stand,_ try_____ to un -der - stand._

Let Love Be Your Energy

words and music by
Robert Williams and Guy Chambers

highest chart position **10**
release date **Monday 9th April 2001**
did you know Robbie recently auctioned a number of personal items (including his kingsize bed and the hand-written lyrics to 'Angels') at Sotheby's in aid of his Give It Sum charity, raising more than £138,000 in the process

(1.) Out of a mil-li-on seeds,_____ on-ly the strong-est one breathes._____
(2.) 'Ev-'ry tear that you cry_____ will be re-placed when you die._____

You made a mi-ra-cle mo-ther, I'll make a man out of me._____
Why don't you love__ your__ bro-ther? Are you out of your mind?_____

Lovin' Each Day

words and music by
Rick Nowels and Gregg Alexander

highest chart position **2**
release date **Monday 16th April 2001**
did you know **The name Ronan means 'baby seal' in Gaelic**

Come on yeah!

We're lov-in' each day as if— it's the last, dan-cin' all night hav-in' a blast.

Ba-by— I need— you here, girl I'm— on a mis-sion to cure my con-

My Girl

words and music by
William Robinson and Ronald White

highest chart position **2 (as B-side of 'What Makes A Man')**
release date **Monday 18th December 2000**
did you know **The first UK magazine article to feature the lads was in 'Boyzone Magazine' September 1998 issue, when they were still known as I.O.YOU and about to support the 'Zone on their tour of Britain and Ireland**

Moderate Rock

I've got

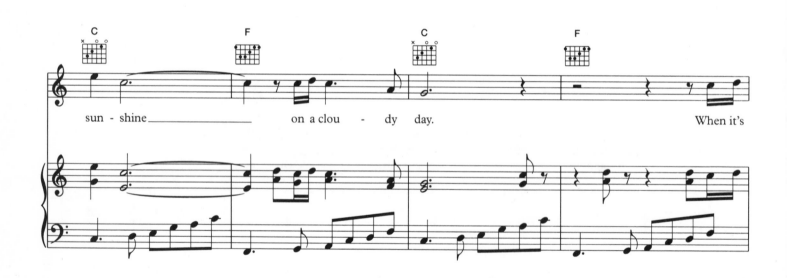

sun - shine _____ on a clou - dy day. When it's

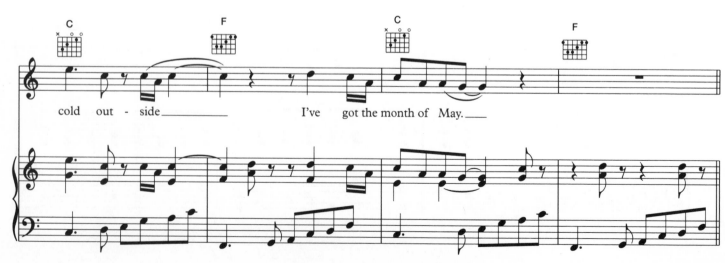

cold out - side _____ I've got the month of May. _____

CODA

New Year

words and music by

Siobhan Donaghy, Mutya Buena, Keisha Buchanan, Cameron McVey, Jony Rockstar, Matt Rowe and Felix Howard

highest chart position **12**
release date **Monday 18th December 2000**
did you know **It was the girls' fondness for sweet-tasting baby food that led to them being called Sugababes**

Love Don't Cost A Thing

words and music by

**Damon Sharpe, George Franklin, Greg Lawson,
Jeremy Monroe and April Harris**

highest chart position 1
release date **Monday 8th January 2001**
did you know Jennifer's debut album 'On The 6' was named after
the train-line she used to take into New York
when she was a young girl

Moderately, with a strong beat ♩ = 96

Think you got-ta keep me iced, you don't. Think I'm gon-na spend your cash, I won't. E-ven if you were broke,_ my love don't cost a

don't.   If I wan-na floss, I got my own.____   E - ven if you were broke,__ my

1. love   don't   cost   a   2. love   don't   cost   a   thing.

Verse 2:
When I took a chance, thought you'd understand,
Baby, credit cards aren't romance.
Still, you're tryin' to buy what's already yours.
What I need from you is not available in stores.
Seen a side of you that I really feel.
You're doin' way too much; never keep it real.
If it doesn't change, gotta hit the road.
Now I'm leavin'. Where's my keys? I've got to go.
(To Pre-Chorus:)

Nobody Wants To Be Lonely

words and music by

Gary Burr, Victoria Shaw and Desmond Child

highest chart position **4**
release date **Monday 26th February 2001**
did you know **To date, Ricky Martin has sold more than 32 million records (over 24 million albums and over 8 million singles) worldwide**

Verse 2:
Can you hear my voice?
Do you hear my song?
It's a serenade
So your heart can find me.
And suddenly you're flying down the stairs
Into my arms, baby.
Before I start going crazy,
Run to me, run to me
'Cause I'm dyin'.
(To Chorus:)

Out Of Reach

words and music by
Gabrielle and Jonathan Shorten

highest chart position 4
release date **Monday 9th April 2001**
did you know This track was chosen above exclusive efforts from
Robbie Williams, Geri Halliwell, Texas and Craig David
as the lead track for the movie 'Bridget Jones's Diary' which is
based on Helen Fielding's internationally best-selling novel

Rendezvous

words and music by
Craig David and Mark Hill

highest chart position 8
release date **Monday 19th March 2001**
did you know Craig called his album 'Born To Do It' after hearing the phrase
in a line from the movie 'Willy Wonka and the Chocolate Factory'

Verse 2:

I'm just sitting here daydreaming about you and all the things you do
Girl feels so right
And all I know is you're the one for me, that special kinda' lady
In my life, in my life.

Well here I am writing you a love song
Holding back those years, it's been so long
And I can't deny the way that I'm feeling (feeling)
It's true, so girl that's why I'm asking you, can we…

Rendezvous *etc.*

No More

highest chart position **6**
release date **Monday 19th February 2001**
did you know **The band have always been involved in music:
Ben was a head chorister at Westminster Abbey as a child,
Christian comes from a family of pop-stars in his native Norway
and Mark represented England at a Romanian Song Festival
winning the Best Young Performer award in the process**

words and music by

Stevie Bensusen, Damon Sharpe, Claudio Cueni and Lindy Robbins

♩=87

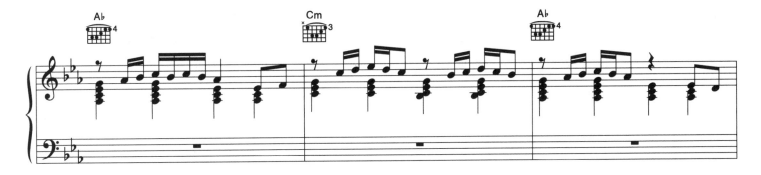

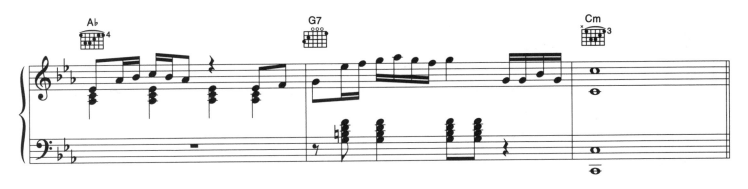

You say you're gon-na work it out, then you say you're hav-in'

Teenage Dirtbag

highest chart position 2
release date **Monday 5th February 2001**
did you know **The Long Island boys' album was recorded in the home of frontman Brendan Brown which led to complaints from neighbours and impromptu dog barking on some of the tracks!**

words and music by
Brendan Brown

Verse lyrics:

1. Her name is No- el, I have a dream a- bout her. She rings my bell got my gym class in half an ho- ur. Oh how she rocks in

2. Her boy-friend's a dick, he brings a gun to school and he'd sim- ply kick my ass if he knew the truth. He lives on my block and he

3. Man I feel like mould it's prom night and I am lone- ly. Lo and be- hold, she's walk-in' ov- er to me, this must be fake my

Too Busy Thinking 'Bout My Baby

words and music by

Barrett Strong, Janie Bradford and Norman Whitfield

highest chart position **2**
(as double A-side with 'The Way You Make Me Feel')
release date **Monday 1st January 2001**
did you know H Steps, whose real name is Ian Watkins,
earned his nickname because of his hyperactive character

I ain't got time to think a-bout mon-ey,

or what it can buy,___ And I ain't got time to

sit down and won - der what makes a bird ___ fly. ___ And I

3. All the diamonds and pearls in the world could never match up to her,
No, no she's some kind of wonderful-people tell you,
I got heaven right here on earth.
I'm just a fella with a one-track mind,
And when it comes to thinkin' 'bout anything but my baby
I just don't have the time.
Oh yeah, and I ain't got time for nothing else.
You know I'm too busy thinkin' 'bout my baby,
And I ain't got time for nothing else –
Too busy thinking about my baby – ain't got time for nothing else, no, no, no,
(Repeat last line and fade)

Supreme

words and music by

**Robert Williams, Guy Chambers,
Dino Fekaris and Frederick Perren**

♩=96

highest chart position **4**
release date **Monday 11th December 2000**
did you know **The three gongs Robbie won at the Brit Awards 2001
(for Best British Male, Best Video and Best British Single)
makes his total haul a record-breaking 12 awards,
including those he won as a member of Take That**

Dm

Dm   Gm7

Oh,   it seemed for - ev - er stopped to - day,___ all the lone-
Oh,   what are you real - ly look-ing for?___ An - oth - er

C   Fmaj7

- ly hearts___ in Lon - don caught a plane___ and flew a - way.___ And all the best
part - ner in your life to a - buse___ and to a - dore?___ Is it love-

Dm/A   E/G#   E7

___ wo - men___ are mar - ried,___ all the hand - some men are gay,___ you feel de -
- ey dov - ey stuff,___ do you need a bit of rough? Get on your knees

Spoken: I spy with my lit-tle eye

some-thing be-gin-ning with. (ah) Got my back up and now she's scream-ing so I've got to turn the track up.

Think About Me

words and music by
Mark Hill and Michelle Escoffrey

highest chart position 11
release date **Monday 5th March 2001**
did you know **Both members of Artful Dodger have a classical background: Mark used to play percussion with the Welsh Philharmonic Orchestra and Pete is a classically trained pianist**

Did you think that you could turn a-way from the love I gave? Did I real-ly hear you say it?

Uptown Girl

words and music by
Billy Joel

highest chart position 1
release date **Monday 5th March 2001**
did you know **This single marks the 24th song to top the charts in two versions (25th if you count Puff Daddy's 'I'll Be Missing You' as an alternative version of the Police's 'Every Breath You Take') and the sixth number one in aid of Comic Relief**

Moderate rock and roll

What It Feels Like For A Girl

words and music by
Madonna Ciccone and Guy Sigsworth

highest chart position **7**
release date **Monday 9th April 2001**
did you know Away from music, Madonna has been put into the 2000 Guinness Book of Records for the most costume changes in a movie for 'Evita'. She changed her costume an amazing 85 times and wore altogether 39 hats, 45 pairs of shoes and 56 pairs of earrings!!

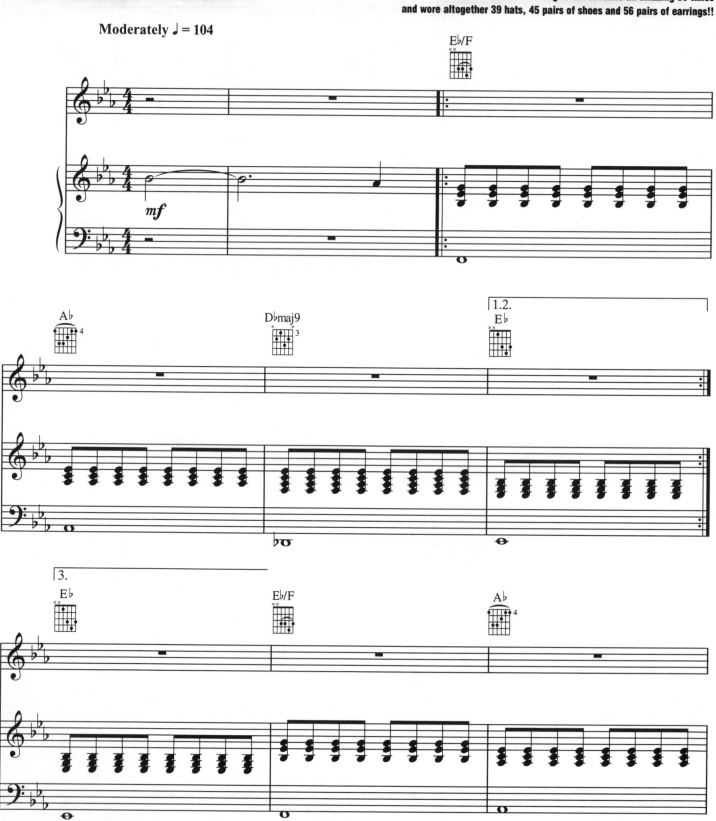

Whole Again

words and music by

**Stuart Kershaw, Andy McCluskey,
Bill Padley and Jeremy Godfrey**

highest chart position 1
release date **Monday 29th January 2001**
did you know **New girl Jenny became friends with the Kittens whilst
touring with her old band Precious, who split up
amicably a while before she got the call to replace Kerry**

You Make Me Sick

words and music by

Obi Nwobosi, Ains Prasad and Marthony Tabb

highest chart position 9
release date **Monday 15th January 2001**
did you know **20-year old Pink can move her neck from side to side (which very few people can do, apparently) and you can see it in the video to her debut UK single 'There You Go'**

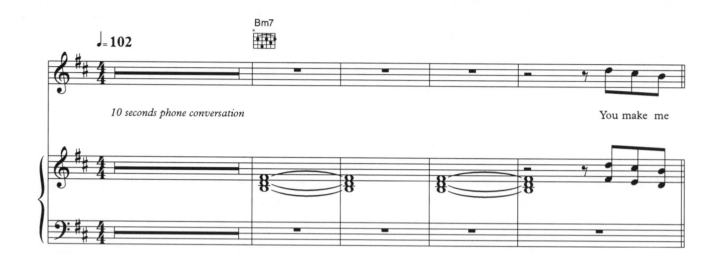

10 seconds phone conversation

You make me

sick. I want you and I'm hat - in' it. ___ Got me lit like a can - dle

stick, get too hot when you touch the tip. ___ I'm feel - in' it, I got - ta get a grip and